who

doing

what

where

to who

describe

when

how

Point to what you see

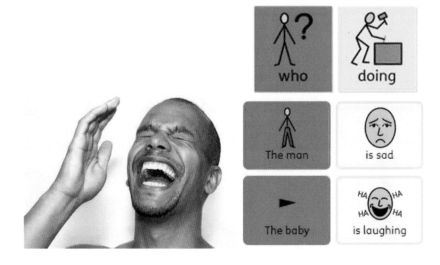

who

doing

The man

is sad

The baby

is laughing

who

doing

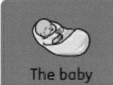
The baby

is swimming

The dog

is sleeping

who 	doing 
The baby 	is swimming 
The dog 	is sleeping

 who	 doing
 The Police Officer	is kicking
 The dog	is smiling

who

doing

The Police Officer

is kicking

The dog

is smiling

who

doing

The cat

is jumping

The lady

is sleeping

who

doing

The cat

is jumping

The lady

is sleeping

who

doing

The horse

is dancing

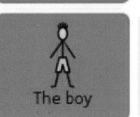

The boy

is hitting

who

doing

The horse

is dancing

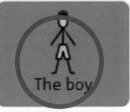
The boy

is hitting

who

doing

The man

is dancing

The girl

is jumping

who

doing

The man

is dancing

The girl

is jumping

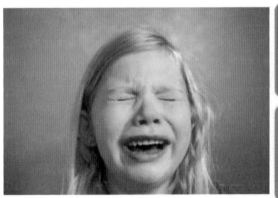

who

doing

The teacher

is running

The girl

is crying

 who	 doing
 The teacher	is running
 The girl	 is crying

 who  doing

 The Dinosaur is falling

 The girl is eating

who | doing

The Dinosaur | is falling

The girl | is eating

who

doing

The Baker

is driving

The Bus Driver

is running

who

doing

The Baker

is driving

The Bus Driver

is running

who

doing

The tiger

is sleeping

The lady

is coughing

who doing

The tiger is sleeping

The lady is coughing

 who

 doing

 The goat

 is running

 The Grandma

 is hitting

who

doing

The goat

is running

The Grandma

is hitting

who

doing

The teacher

is hiding

The Grandma

is singing

who

doing

The teacher

is hiding

The Grandma

is singing

The End

Printed in Great Britain
by Amazon

40673774R00016